AF481128

KNOW
THYSELF.
MIND.

KNOW THYSELF. MIND.

Transforming challenges to opportunities

OlenaOM

Library of Congress Control Number: 2024920944

ISBN: 979-8-89228-227-7   (Paperback)
ISBN: 979-8-89228-228-4   (Hardcover)
ISBN: 979-8-89228-229-1   (eBook)

ZOOMing MIND

Printed in the United States of America

Our Times: Engaged in Self-Deception

In our era, self-deception is widespread. To truly understand this brief exploration, one must employ analytical thinking and a critical perspective on life—seeing both sides of the coin, or, as it were, the stick with two ends.

When we know, we know. There's no need for guessing, believing, or regretting; we learn, step by step, day by day. Life unfolds in the present moment.

Consider this: if given a vehicle or a new device as a gift, its usefulness depends on our understanding of how to use it. Without knowing how, its value diminishes. A phone is no hammer, and a computer is useless without a manual or a connection to Wi-Fi. The same principle applies to life's tools and gifts.

I've pondered many questions: Who are we? Where do we come from? Where do we go after physical existence? What is the purpose of it all? Why do some seem happy while others struggle? Why do marriages start with love and end in hatred? Why are some healthy while others fall ill?

Raised in fear of God and life, I sought answers. Frustration often drives us to seek and develop—if we don't give up or blame the world for our troubles.

Imagine a world where everyone lives in harmony, giving only good advice with genuine smiles! To return to unity, to the endless symphony of existence, is to comprehend the eternal laws of life. Our thoughts, as energy, shape our worlds. They can bring storms or gentle rains, depending on how we manage them.

Love and sincerity are foundational. By embodying our best selves and reflecting our inner bliss, we influence the world positively. Our lessons and challenges are opportunities to cultivate the right thoughts, which in turn manifest in our reality.

Becoming conscious of our ever-active MIND means guarding against negative thoughts that can cloud our judgment. Mother Earth, our material plane, and our bodies are our temporary vessels. Self-consciousness involves creating and nurturing thoughts with intention, maintaining a disciplined MIND to harvest goodwill and true fortune.

Great expectations lead to great outcomes. Applying knowledge daily and directing our energy thoughtfully improves our lives and aligns us with our dreams. We are divine operators, shaping our reality with conscious intention.

Fear and stress stem from misunderstanding; they are illusions. Our thoughts and emotions shape our experiences, and our desires must be monitored carefully. The body is our vehicle—ensure it's well-maintained and directed wisely.

Wisdom lies in understanding how to operate this powerful system. Words have the power to uplift or diminish us. God does not punish us; our MINDS can be our greatest allies or our worst enemies. We have the freedom to choose our path, to tune into harmony and growth.

Reflect and project, unwinding into new realities like a butterfly. Just as we MINDS our daily nourishment, we must also care for our mental state. Create and embrace positive, juicy thoughts!

Examining the MINDS reveals the true quality of life. What thoughts serve us? What patterns, habits, and beliefs shape our existence? Life's reflection is a mirror of our inner self.

Evolution means gradual improvement, while devolution is a path of corruption and lost potential. Those living in darkness, self-doubt, or without compassion struggle. Structured thoughts and data guide our life path; learning and adapting are essential.

Living in joy, love, and hope contrasts with the fear and greed that lead to suffering. Return to truth by cutting out the roots of evil. Living in constant fear results in dis-ease and abnormality.

Temporal pain is natural; stay conscious of your experiences and gratitude. Reflect on the blessings in your life, and let spiritual discernment guide you to freedom.

Summon the courage, willpower, and determination to master your life. Awaken to the truth and act decisively. We all have the potential to lead fulfilling lives. By observing how our MINDS are constantly processing thoughts—whether constructive or destructive—we can command our MINDS to navigate us toward our desired destination.

To achieve true fulfillment, spiritual strength is essential. Embrace thoughts that are noble and inspiring, creating a clear path with ease and gratification.

Everything we see is a gift freely given: the rising sun, flowing rivers, vast oceans, and fresh air—all freely provided. The greatest gift of all is our precious presence, illuminated by the stars and the minerals of the earth.

When the light is on, darkness vanishes. Illuminate your soul's essence, and the brighter the light, the clearer your vision. Follow your passions, whether they come swiftly or slowly, reflecting nature's radiance. Relations and collaborations flow in and out, as above, so below.

All that is free is created by the Creator, fueled by love's impulse— Nature's alchemist! Here on this beautiful, bountiful Mother Earth, everything we create comes from existing resources: food, glass, metals—all provided by nature. We didn't create water or milk, but we transform nature's elements—grain, water, salt— into bread. This process of taking, acting, and creating is how we interact with the world.

We are souls wearing material "robes" to experience life. While we live in the same world, our perception and experience depend on how we set our MINDS: constructively or destructively. A hat or any man-made tool begins as a creative thought, embodying the idea that "as above, so below"—people create and become truly rich!

Therefore, we must be mindful of what we create. Discipline the MINDS to focus on what nurtures us. Just as we welcome friends into our homes, we should carefully consider the quality of thoughts we allow into our MINDS. Our bodies are our personal sanctuaries; the quality of our thoughts directly influences our choices, actions, and outcomes.

Gradually improving our thoughts and understanding how they shape our lives leads to renewal and strength. We were born in love, and love desires union and connection. When encountering those who are like children—fearful or complaining—treat them with the same compassion we'd offer a child, guiding them by example.

Even if our earthly parents didn't always show their love, their gift of life is enough. We can always seek and find new paths. Heaven is not a place; it is a state of being. As students and teachers, we must improve our inner state and connect our vital, psychic, and physical energies.

Our hair, nails, and every cell have memory. Each focus or impression leaves an imprint on our subconscious MINDS. We inherit cell-memory through our lineage and childhood, which may include both healthy beliefs and fears. Consciously awaken from automatic reactions, cultivating positive habits and self-talk. Reflect your inner world in your external reality—this is mind-body harmony.

Intellect, spirituality, ethics, and morality shape our expectations. Each of us can ascend or descend on the ladder of existence. Climbing requires strength and effort, while descending is easier. Like salmon swimming upstream to lay eggs before returning to the ocean, we must face our challenges to grow stronger.

Old habits often overpower new ideas. It takes time and discipline to develop constructive learning skills and achieve meaningful results. Self-improvement is challenging for those who lack true maturity and awareness. Acting without love leads us to the opposite end of the duality ladder—hate. Repeating actions that bring boredom or complaint may seem as if an external force is controlling our lives. In reality, everything lies within us; thoughts have energy.

A positive, constructive mindset is a skill we can develop, enriching our lives and aligning us with the universe's harmony.

By the universal laws of gravitation and similarity, what we reflect upon tends to multiply. Those who awaken don't need to read about morality; it is embedded in our very being. When we harness our inner power and direct our genius MINDS to create with love and respect for others, our generous intentions flourish, and happiness abounds.

Every religion, in its own way, points to the same ultimate truth: love, light, and unity. Imagine the world as a vast hill that we've all been climbing since the beginning. In the darkness, amidst struggles and competing trails, each of us carries the same ancient essence in our veins—our personal and ancestral history.

Within our spirits lies innate knowledge, a sense of moral goodness, and obligation to do right. This inner wisdom guides us in choosing what is good for ourselves and others, affirming our free will.

Mother Earth and Father Spirit guide our souls to uncover deeper mysteries. Yet, in the depths of darkness, it's hard to see. Fear and guilt, rooted in our MINDS, arise from a lack of harmony with our thoughts. Our MINDS, when properly focused and guided, can avoid feelings of depression, worry, or envy. Like a taxi, our MINDS Sneed a clear destination to navigate us effectively.

Constant complainers often lack a heartfelt destination. They are unaware of their true selves and the fruits of their actions. Thoughts that bring darkness are rooted in our history and subconscious. Yet, we can awaken to a new self by choosing a path of co-creation with a higher spirit. Through our will, we master and embody our purpose, evolving into creative, joyful, and enlightened souls within the material world.

This transformation is gradual, requiring effort and thoughtful learning, much like a plant growing towards the sun. Our true selves seek nourishment—positive thoughts and information that enrich our inner formation and update our mental software.

We all have the essence of "I am." As infants, we may not recall our names, but we instinctively know our existence. Although parents love and care for us, each child adapts to the faces and beliefs around them, which may be pleasant or otherwise. Born into a complex world, we inherit a mix of lifestyles and qualities.

We are born naked, donning the "costume" of the body. Just as animals exhibit collective qualities—strength in lions, keen vision in eagles, loyalty in dogs, or grace in cats—we reflect the qualities designed by our spirit. Our inner, mental world mirrors our outer reality, from spirit to material form.

People have many theories, but what truly matters is how we design and create, understanding both strengths and weaknesses from micro to macro. As seasons change and people respond, our focus and intention bear fruit.

We all come from the Edenic realm, where duality and unity are intertwined. The   of "I am" is a new creation, evolving with time and seasons. Our souls, guided by spiritual light and wisdom, become powerful and radiant.

As stated, "Ask, and it shall be given to you; seek, and you shall find; knock, and it shall be opened unto you." Thoughts that remain unspoken are unheard; words without action are merely words. Formulated thoughts, when expressed and acted upon, yield results—either poison or divine substance. Hence, it is crucial to align our thoughts, words, and deeds.

When our MINDS are clear and pure, life flows like a pristine spring. In the animal kingdom, fear is natural; in the human world, those possessed by darkness also experience fear. Ignorance of light and natural laws leads to pretense and confusion about saying "no." Unfinished plans and promises must be resolved with peace of MIND and trust, for we are the architects of our destinies.

We are the authors of our lives, responsible for all effects and outcomes. Challenges and difficulties point us toward better decisions, enabling us to master our lives and excel in every experience. By optimizing and managing our personal growth, we become the best versions of ourselves—mentally stable, emotionally healthy, and renewed.

Thus, we build happier families and peaceful nations, fostering collective joy and cooperative cultural achievements.

• •

Aggression is a behavior intended to cause emotional or physical harm. **Fear-inducing news** often creates false evidence that seems real, making us vulnerable, defensive, and prone to feelings of guilt, shame, doubt, depression, or **emotional**, mental, and physical harm.

It's crucial to **identify the source** of our actions and act only from inspired ideas, deliberately researched and analyzed. When we comprehend the **results** of our actions, we create improvement for **all** involved—upgrading, renovating, beautifying, and achieving betterment. Quality should be measured both subjectively and objectively, blending **personal** feelings with factual evidence.

- **Subjective** **views** are based on individual opinions or feelings, reflecting **personal** perspectives.

- **Objective views** are grounded in facts, free from **personal** bias.

Intellectual arrogance is overconfidence in one's beliefs, abilities, and knowledge—often manifesting as narcissism. **Divinity** is the state of being that can be felt but not seen, embodying the **essence** of the Holy Spirit.

Intelligence is **knowing** what to do and being able to do it. **Radiance** reflects good mental, **emotional**, and vital health, **inner** strength, trust, and a confident, joyful glow.

Morality without spirituality leads to abnormality. It becomes a world of duality—right versus wrong, fight or flight. A spiritually enlightened individual can achieve higher levels of development, manifesting positive change and **growth**. Spirituality does not imply religiosity. Religious texts are often allegorical, containing symbolic narratives that reveal hidden meanings, where characters represent moral qualities.

Every human has two inclinations: one pulling upward, the other downward. We must ask ourselves, "What qualities do I want to embody? What is my perspective on life?" Our perception drives our thinking, decisions, and actions. Words carry energy for action, shaping both form and content.

Instead of asking "Why is it broken?" we can ask, "How can it function better?" This shift in perspective opens the MINDS to genius solutions. Ask yourself: "How can I improve? What have I long desired? What is the best plan for resolving this issue?" Affirming our abilities—"I am able! I can do this! It is possible!"—leads to new directions and destinations.

Understanding complex things can be simple when we apply the right approach and maintain a peaceful, mindful state. By asking the right questions, ideas begin to materialize, revealing their form from invisible concepts. This is the design of our true nature and uniqueness, expanding our opportunities.

The MIND can be trained to think constructively, serving our conscious directions. It's a choice, a matter of determination, and individual experience. We can choose a destination and joyfully pursue it daily, creating a life rich with opportunities. In doing so, we accept our sovereign nature, spiritually attuned and equal to others. We don't get angry at our cat when we're mad; similarly, we shouldn't let anger control us, as it only leads to more unwanted situations.

When the MIND lacks meaningful tasks or goals, it goes astray. We must be the coachman of our own MINDS, guiding them to where we intend to go. Life on Earth is an amazing gift, a self-awareness mission of consciousness.

Self-realization is a transformative power that awakens our ability to perceive and feel our thoughts and emotions. When we are on the right path, our conscience is at peace, leading to a happy state of MIND.

Anger signals opposition to evil, a call to rebuild or restructure. Just as old buildings may need demolition to make room for new ones, anger can be a force for necessary change.

All reality is consciousness experiencing itself in a divine play. Art, words, and symbols are the structure of thought, related to wisdom, intelligence, integrity, and courage. We must balance physical and metaphysical equilibrium, understanding that the visible is in proportion to the invisible. Stability and motion, progress and necessity, justice and mercy—all are interconnected.

Wisdom is the strength to watch oneself and achieve victory. We are creators, and through self-improvement, we change our inner selves, which in turn changes the world around us. Life is always in motion, shaped by our mental filters. Liberation and light come through our focus and energy.

When we observe or think about something, we amplify its energy. We must learn to identify our true intentions and the results they bring. Not everything happens randomly; some things have a purpose. By correcting our beliefs, we can optimize our lives and excel in service to others and the Earth.

Ask yourself, "Who am I? How do I express myself to the world? How am I in my own MIND?" Create a new strategic thinking partnership with your MIND, blending love, excitement, and gratitude into your thoughts. As you gradually change your views, your opportunities will change too—that's a law of physics and philosophy.

We have freedom over our own thinking, but we are also influenced by others. When we are not firm, we may be swayed by toxic influences, leading to distraction, disease, or unnecessary disturbances. We can identify a consonant melody and distinguish the bad smell of rotten food. Our intuition, our divine device, gives us clear signals. When we focus on or involve ourselves in any endeavor, we march toward failure or victory, depending on where it leads. Our character is cultivated by our thoughts.

We attract our fears, but we can learn to live without chronic fear, focusing instead on excelling in mindful, graceful responses. A well-tended garden grows beautiful fruits, while a neglected one attracts weeds and pests. Be a good gardener of your thoughts, cultivating them with patience, enthusiasm, and persistence.

By the universal laws of gravitation and similarity, what we reflect upon tends to multiply. Those who awaken don't need to read about morality; it is embedded in our very being. When we harness our inner power and direct our genius MIND to create with love and respect for others, our generous intentions flourish, and happiness abounds.

Every religion, in its own way, points to the same ultimate truth: love, light, and unity. Imagine the world as a vast hill that we've all been climbing since the beginning. In the darkness, amidst struggles and competing trails, each of us carries the same ancient essence in our veins—our personal and ancestral history.

Within our spirits lies innate knowledge, a sense of moral goodness and obligation to do right. This inner wisdom guides us in choosing what is good for ourselves and others, affirming our free will.

Mother Earth and Father Spirit guide our souls to uncover deeper mysteries. Yet, in the depths of darkness, it's hard to see. Fear and guilt, rooted in our MINDS, arise from a lack of harmony with our thoughts. Our MINDS, when properly focused and guided, can avoid feelings of depression, worry, or envy. Like a taxi, our MINDS Sneed a clear destination to navigate us effectively.

Constant complainers often lack a heartfelt destination. They are unaware of their true selves and the fruits of their actions. Thoughts that bring darkness are rooted in our history and subconscious. Yet, we can awaken to a new self by choosing a path of co-creation with a higher spirit. Through our will, we master and embody our purpose, evolving into creative, joyful, and enlightened souls within the material world.

This transformation is gradual, requiring effort and thoughtful learning, much like a plant growing towards the sun. Our true selves seek nourishment—positive thoughts and information that enrich our inner formation and update our mental software.

We all have the essence of "I am." As infants, we may not recall our names, but we instinctively know our existence. Although parents love and care for us, each child adapts to the faces and beliefs around them, which may be pleasant or otherwise. Born into a complex world, we inherit a mix of lifestyles and qualities.

We are born naked, donning the "costume" of the body. Just as animals exhibit collective qualities—strength in lions, keen vision in eagles, loyalty in dogs, or grace in cats—we reflect the qualities designed by our spirit. Our inner, mental world mirrors our outer reality, from spirit to material form.

People have many theories, but what truly matters is how we design and create, understanding both strengths and weaknesses from micro to macro. As seasons change and people respond, our focus and intention bear fruit.

We all come from the Edenic realm, where duality and unity are intertwined. The essence of "I am" is a new creation, evolving with time and seasons. Our souls, guided by spiritual light and wisdom, become powerful and radiant.

As stated, "Ask, and it shall be given to you; seek, and you shall find; knock, and it shall be opened unto you." Thoughts that remain unspoken are unheard; words without action are merely words. Formulated thoughts, when expressed and acted upon, yield results—either poison or divine substance. Hence, it is crucial to align our thoughts, words, and deeds.

When our MINDS are clear and pure, life flows like a pristine spring. In the animal kingdom, fear is natural; in the human world, those possessed by darkness also experience fear. Ignorance of light and natural laws leads to pretense and confusion about saying "no." Unfinished plans and promises must be resolved with peace of MIND and trust, for we are the architects of our destinies.

We are the authors of our lives, responsible for all effects and outcomes. Challenges and difficulties point us toward better decisions, enabling us to master our lives and excel in every experience. By optimizing and managing our personal growth, we become the best versions of ourselves—mentally stable, emotionally healthy, and renewed.

Thus, we build happier families and peaceful nations, fostering collective joy and cooperative cultural achievements.

Every situation is like a unique soup, with special ingredients that make it what it is. To bake perfect bread, the right balance of flour and water, adequate rising time, and the correct temperature are essential. Similarly, in life, we can gather inspiration, learn, and act—or we can procrastinate and blame others. Complaints about the world or others often reflect an unwillingness to take responsibility for our own choices.

Big or small plans require structure. Using the wrong ingredients or timing will result in an unsatisfactory outcome. With a well-developed, calm, and reasonable character, we can attain a state of stable happiness. True cohesion happens when all parts fit together harmoniously.

Imagine Earth as an egg, with the yolk as its core. The white layer represents the air, and the shell is the sky. Our pure awareness of perception is like the sky—boundless and open. Our natural perception is joy and bliss, untainted by conceptual thought. It exists beyond the limits of presence and absence, calm and movement. Our continuous perception is a constant flow of meditation, limitless and indivisible, existing without rush or vanity.

Today, on Sunday, the seventh day, I ponder the nature of good and evil. Have we ever truly seen them? Everything in the world, good or evil, has been created by people. We are at the center of duality. Every moment, our thoughts and feelings shape our state of being, attracting energies that resonate with us, whether toward heaven or hell. We can either run from fear or shine our inner light, guiding others fearlessly.

The only true enemy is feeding energy into nightmares—unconscious fears, doubts, and anger that weaken us. History shows us the consequences of such fears: emotional constipation, destructive patterns, and lost civilizations. Like a wrecked car driver, we reveal our immaturity and carelessness when we let ourselves be driven by darkness. By choosing happiness and setting an example, we contribute to a world of joy and harmony.

Our souls, like our breath, are always present. If something smells bad, we know it's not right. If we consume spoiled food, our bodies will react. Similarly, if we consume negative information, it affects us. A spiritually awake person will avoid harmful influences and recognize their power to shape a better world.

Health and clarity come from using the right tools and habits. As we develop strength through mental discipline, we choose to believe in good over evil. As stated in Matthew 6:24, "No man can serve two masters: for either he will hate the one and love the other; or else he will hold to one and despise the other. You cannot serve God and mammon."

Just as adding something undesirable ruins a meal, our qualities define our essence. We are already connected through the centuries of blood and energy flowing through us. Mastering our inner powers involves the process of transmutation—changing and refining ourselves. Earth is our plane for learning and conversion. By separating the essential from the non-essential, we purify our experience.

Humans are unique in their ability to laugh and bring joy. While animals live with natural fear, we have the potential to be counselors and bringers of joy. Understanding leads to faith and well-being, allowing us to create and express ourselves fully. We are bearers of joy, dancing through life with devotion and commitment.

"In the world, not of the world," joyful energies vitalize our being. Fear paralyzes, while love and understanding foster growth and connection. Treat others as you wish to be treated, respecting their uniqueness. Just as there are diverse flowers and fruits, we each have our own path. Let yourself live authentically and allow others to do the same. On the emotional scale, we measure our stability or instability in relation to ourselves, our families, and our energy exchanges.

From love and connection to dislike and passionate hate, our emotional state reflects our inner world and interactions.

Understanding leads to faith, a knowing that brings ease and well-being. In this state, you can create, devoted and committed, a bringer of **growth** and well-being for all. You become a bearer of joy, a blissful dancer in the rhythm of life.

"In the world, not of the world," your joyful energy vitalizes the body, while fear only paralyzes. Treat others as you wish to be treated—without dictating how they should live or suppressing their spirit. We are each unique, as varied as the flowers in a field, as diverse as the fruits of the earth.

Allow yourself to live the life you choose, and grant others the freedom to be themselves. **Emotions**, like a temperature gauge, reveal our stability or instability, reflecting how we relate to ourselves, to family, to the energy of income and outcome. From **love** to indifference, from dislike to revolution, even to passionate hate—each emotion marks a point on our internal scale.

illustrate this

From profound	1. Joy, knowledge, empowerment, freedom, **love**, appreciation.
VICTORY	2. Passion.
	3. Enthusiasm, interest
Upward	4. Positive expectation, belief.
Spiral	5. Optimism
	6. Hopefulness
	7. Contentment
Downward:	8. Boredom.
	9. Pessimism.

Spiral

10. Frustration, irritation, impatience.

11. Overwhelming.

12. Disappointment.

13. Doubt.

14. Worry.

15. Blame. 16. Discouragement.

17. Anger. 18. Revenge. 19. Hatred/rage.
20. Jealousy.

21. Insecurity Guilt/Unworthiness

22. Fear/Grief/Depression/
Powerlessness/ VICTIM

Here we are. All our actions stem from our state of being. At any moment, we are either evolving or regressing, a chain reaction at the subtle level of consciousness. We can lead this process only if we are aware of it. We are meant to evolve spiritually, in harmony with our technological advancements. Think positive, empowering thoughts. When connected to the cosmic spiritual source, we can live with compassionate intelligence and common sense, creating peaceful, focused communities. A spark of cosmic light—*LIFE*—resides within us all. We are each a fractal of one brilliant Source, sons and daughters of the mighty.

Like one body with many systems and functions, each of us has a purpose, serving the whole. How can one cell hate another in the same body? If it does, the entire system, or parts of it, suffer—resulting in crisis, tension, impaired judgment. Each of us is important, serving a higher purpose when our spiritual, mental, emotional, and physical well-being is in balance. Seek knowledge and apply it daily; it is food for the soul. If we don't feed the fire, it will go out. We must tend to our flame, keep oil in our lamps—this is the Holy Spirit. Without it, we cannot move forward.

Be mindful of the Holy Spirit, love, and goodwill. Cooperation and the mastery of wise inner qualities are what it means to become truly human—rising above the animal MIND, moving closer to perfection, away from distortions. The answers are within us. Every problem has a solution. With higher awareness, you'll count your blessings, and they will multiply, enhancing the quality of your daily life in a beautiful sequence.

We have limited time on this journey. It's vital to wake up and realise our essence while we are here. Establish your individual identity and master your unique qualities. What world do you belong to, vibrate with, and serve? Do you still harbour great fears greater than your good expectations? Do you still see enemies? Check the energies. Good expectations and supportive thoughts inspire actions that lead to positive outcomes, finished creations, and evolution.

All good and evil occur within us, in each person. Those who are alive and awake see the potential. We could become ever-happy nations, an avant-garde, evolved, humane civilisation. Joy, serenity, renewed energy, and unrelenting happiness—this is progress.

Realise your intent and purpose. Be aware of what your unattended MIND is thinking. Have you given it a command to create by your own will, prudently directed? What is the quality and direction of your thoughts? How do you speak to yourself and others? Do you treat those you love with respect, gentleness, and care? How would you truly treat the ones you love? Heal and craft an integrated life.

Energy can turn into matter, and matter into energy. Become an energy millionaire. Live 24 hours a day in positive thinking. It's beneficial not only for your psychological and physical well-being but also for protecting you from negative influences. One negative thought can affect many, but positive thinking dilutes fear, heartache, hopelessness, sadness, and sorrow, making life easier for all of us.

Begin by working on your thoughts, words, and most-used phrases. Step out of the game of fear and guilt. When we react calmly, we stay at our potential. We don't lose ourselves in the storm. Destructive situations grow thinner and eventually disappear. And most pleasantly, your situation resolves in the best way. This is the highest law of the universe.

Releasing bad habits and adopting new, healthy ones takes time and inner effort. These habits will bring integrity, passion, commitment, strength, and courage. Is your self-talk filled with doubts about your worthiness? Change your mindset to a positive one, and life will improve automatically.

Check a few times a day—do you have a happy smile on your face, and do those around you smile as well?

Appreciate yourself, knowing you are worthy and deserving. Live with love. When entering a new situation, see how love paves the way. Be willing to change your approach. Your inner light will allow you to see the world with new eyes, helping you learn something new every day. Choose to know the truth. Open your **inner** **vision**, grow stronger and deeper, and see through deception. Rise up—wisdom is your birthright. We **all** have unique talents and capabilities. Trust your intuition; it's your gut feeling guiding you. Complete what needs to be finished so you can move forward.

A whole new world awaits, a new path to take. But first, clear the way. Put endings on what needs to be finished, so you're not dragging old energy forward. Transformation, rebirth, and **creation**—plant the **seeds** you want to grow. Look ahead to how you'll nurture them to maturity.

Maybe you need more education, more specific knowledge, or the support of certain people in your life. Togetherness, trust, and an increase in strength, confidence, and courage will help you grow. Increase harmony in giving and receiving **love** with sincerity and honesty. We **all** grow in stages. Acceptance and exploration are natural on the path of evolution. We **all** start as fools and grow towards mastery.

When we accept where we are and do our best with **love**, attention to detail, and happiness, life moves us forward. We grow stronger and earn our place. In contrast, when we resist, complain, and envy others, everything becomes more complicated and difficult. Life reflects our attitude—smile at the mirror, and it smiles back.

Healthy **MINDS** create healthy bodies. Avoid vanity and empty talk—they are bad company. Feeling well as a habit keeps our endorphin levels high, allowing us to stay in a state of vitality, enduring life's challenges with ease.

Everything we do must be felt deeply. When we eat, **focus** on the food to better taste the richness of life. Little things and good habits matter; they affect long-term **results**. Prioritise trust, unity, and **creation**. Reboot your system—release old burdens, shift towards healthy pleasures, and forgive yourself for past shame.

There is no life in tension, no development. Tension blocks the divine flow within us, creating pressure in our veins. Let energy flow freely. Our environment reflects what we broadcast and transmit. See the big picture, live playfully, treat others equally, and create a beautiful game of life.

Let new codes download into your system. You'll begin to see more possibilities, more beauty, more abundance than you ever allowed yourself to see before. The quality of your communications and relationships will brighten, deepen, and become more loving—on both a cosmic and earthly level.

Build new structures, activate new neural networks, and embrace a new way of perceiving and creating. Healing restores the original structure, creating a new crystal framework where you manifest your highest potential in radiant vibration.

Get ready. Enjoy **creation** with divine **love**, interest, playfulness, and adventure, realising your infinite potential in the **present moment**.

Hard people soften, soft people strengthen. It takes great courage and devotion to the truth. Don't lie to yourself, don't lie to others—it takes courage and a deep awareness of energy intensity and vibration frequencies.

Father God is not punishing us; He created universal laws.

There are natural laws we must recognise and understand:

1. **The Cosmic Law of Unity in Diversity:**

    "The universe is an organised system of correlated and coordinated parts, forming a true unity."

2. **The Cosmic Law of Activity:**

    "Everything is in constant motion. The cosmos is alive with activity, movement, and energy. There is an underlying, all-pervading activity in the cosmos as a whole, and within each of its parts."

3. **The Cosmic Law of Change:**

    "Everything changes; nothing is permanent. The cosmos, in its entirety and in each of its components, is in constant flux. Time itself is but measured change, with continuity and orderly sequence flowing in a **continuous** stream."

4. **The Cosmic Law of Causation:**

    "Everything happens for a reason. **observer All** changes in the cosmos are conditioned and caused. They manifest, proceed, and eventually fade through the influence of these conditioning causes."

5. **The Cosmic Law of Rhythm or Periodicity:**

"Everything moves in rhythmic cycles. All cosmic activities follow measured rhythms, cycles, and periodic succession. Involution always precedes evolution—two contrasting poles of a single great process."

6. **The Cosmic Law of Polarity:**

"Everything exists as a pair of opposites. The cosmos manifests polarity in all its parts, where each quality has its opposite. These pairs of opposites form two contrasting poles of a greater unity."

7. **The Cosmic Law of Balance or Compensation:**

"All things are balanced. The activities of the cosmos are in equilibrium, manifesting a state of balance and counterbalance."

From the beginning, we are part of this grand design. Recognising our place within it brings enlightenment, and everything falls into its rightful place. We are all "I ams," the conscious awareness that knows when we sleep, when we are happy, and when we are not. This inner observer is the centre of our being, ever-present and independent of our physical body. The MIND, with its temporary nature, cannot fully comprehend this emptiness that contains the timeless totality.

We are like actors on a stage, wearing costumes and playing roles. When we return home, we take off our robes. In the midst of the play, we forget that we are merely actors, becoming deeply entangled in the drama. But life is a series of chapters, each with its own scenario. We play our parts, take breaks, and continue the story. Each of us is the hero of our own production, with main and supporting actors. Every night, we return to our true family as we sleep. At the end of the movie, we depart, returning home to reflect on our performance. Some create beautiful stories with happy endings, while others become lost in the seriousness of the play, forgetting it is only a temporary role.

In our bodies, **growth** factor receptors are the first stop where the signalling cascade for cell differentiation and proliferation begins. Just as healthy cells are essential for the body's function, healthy MINDS are crucial for a healthy civilisation. Harmony, cooperation, and trust are the foundations of a healthy MIND. **Creation** becomes possible when we consciously connect and harmonise with the energy around us.

We must be able to differentiate the energies we encounter. Are these feelings our own, or do they belong to others? In the past, mass understanding of energy was slow to develop, but as we evolve, we gain clarity. **Creation** and duality function within the **material** world, like a single life—a one-time movie production. Energy is the life particle within us, with the body as its extension. When we expand our perception, viewing life from a spherical awareness, we see past, **present**, and future simultaneously. This expanded perspective allows us to look at ourselves and our situations with new eyes.

Feelings of loneliness are a longing for the true self, while sadness and isolation stem from   conflict. These conflicts may not even be our own but could be inherited from our family, our neighbours, or our country's history. We must ask ourselves: *Is this mine? Is this belief still relevant?* By scanning the energies we allow into our MINDS, we can better structure our lives.

Everyone has a specific field of energy around them. Depression, for instance, is a deprivation, a cutting off from the natural flow of energy—the Source of all. It is separation. All is energy; we must discern the divine from the distorted.

What version of ourselves do we wish to be? We can align ourselves with empathetic coherence, on a cellular and quantum level, vibrationally matching the energies we attract into our magnetic field.

Energy in Formation

Within us, two energies reside—Yin and Yang. Yang is action, the force of doing and realisation. Yin is rest, the nurturing fullness that saturates and sustains. Like father and mother, these energies converge to create the unique "me." This "one unique me" connects with its opposite to create another "unique other." When opposites cooperate, intertwining in harmony, they create something new, something beautiful and greater.

But when opposites fall into disassociation, disharmony, and competition, they disconnect—leading to divorce, war, and chaos. We must change our characters, cleanse ourselves of anger, envy, and hate. To evolve, we must become more honest, kind, and aligned with our true nature. Civilisations have been swept from the earth for failing these tests. We now stand at a crossroads, facing tests of humanity, integrity, and sincerity. Even the devil despises those who sin, so why serve the wicked when their destiny is dust?

We will encounter evil and injustice—tests of our honesty, our ability to resist deceit, and our capacity to avoid betrayal. How greedy are we? Do we deceive others for our own gain? Do we gossip, slander, or blame others for our troubles? It is easier to blame another than to accept responsibility for adversity, but decency requires self-reflection. Do we lie, act dishonestly, or believe lies to be true? These are tests of our integrity, our willingness to trade our loved ones for fleeting gains.

Anger, irritation, and hate lead us to downfall. Slandering others blinds us to the truth, making it impossible to make righteous decisions. We are all equal—there is no pride, no vanity here. The old world is crumbling; heavy emotions weigh us down. Only those who cleanse themselves of these burdens will rise. Those who cling to fear and refuse to change will suffer and be tormented by their own illusions. Some fear to look within, trapped in the lies they tell themselves. But we must face our true selves.

Wisdom and knowledge are not the same. Knowing many things does not make one wise. Each person has their own opinion, their own choices, and each is responsible for their actions—whether constructive or destructive.

The soul is a fragment of the spirit, with a divine beginning. Spiritual growth is the process by which the soul learns to control its body, to master its emotions, and to live a life of love and purpose. "Love what you do, and do what you love." This is the path to the Higher Spirit, the connection to your essence, the Divine Beginning, and spiritual ascent. We are here to gain new knowledge, experience, and development. Many civilisations have passed through this before us, and many will follow.

No one is punishing us—we refine ourselves. This circle of refinement is nearing its end. We are at the point of separating the wheat from the chaff, as the Bible says. The wheat represents those truly repentant, delivered from evil, and freed from sin. We have a finite amount of time on this earth, living in our avatar bodies, our garments. The essence is that we build our own life and destiny. We know not all that glitters is gold.

The material world is the domain of the devil, while the spiritual world is the realm of the Absolute. Only by connecting the human with the spirit do we become whole, evolved beings. Tangible connected to intangible. Our bodies are energy batteries, and beyond physics, there are other energies, forces, and parallel realities. Without fear, we can explore what is good and what is evil on this spiral of evolution. Religion, for some, is a tool; for others, a toy. The God waiting on a throne to judge us is a misinterpretation. The Bible is a story of both the most evil and the most saintly. Its knowledge is encoded in parables and allegories.

"Those who have eyes to see will see, and those who have ears to hear will hear." If we participate in evil, even for a price, we are part of it. Joy is fleeting, but happiness is a long-term state of being. Joy is an emotion we can choose to create lasting happiness. And Jesus enhances your consultations.

"Nothing unclean shall enter the New Jerusalem—Heaven." This is a spiritual principle: "Nothing unclean, nothing with the stain of sin, will enter Heaven." We can create high-quality, lasting goods and a new way of living. What we tell ourselves will manifest. Our habitual thoughts are the seeds we plant, and the soil will grow whatever we sow—be it weeds or fruitful crops. By achieving,

not avoiding, we let go of judgment and live with effortless ease. Enjoy every step of your journey—this beautiful, magical journey unfolding before us. We have eternity.

Raising our **consciousness** and awareness elevates our vitality, shifting everything. You don't need to take from others to feel well; allow your own abundance to flow. Integrate every part of yourself. But many have limited beliefs about their self-worth. This is the greatest time to be here, to be part of this great awakening of human **consciousness**. Every single one of us is divine **love**, an eternal presence. Spirituality is a **personal** journey.

Embrace your life. Get practical, get grounded to the earth. Kick off your shoes and touch the mother earth. Maintain alignment and clarity. Understand where you may sabotage yourself. Think about your inspirations, your talents, and simplify your plans. Determine what you will do next. Identify what perceptions may be blocking your path. You have talents—how will you take them to the next level? Mastery is your destiny. Rise with dignity.

The stream of energy is powerful. Coincidences happen when we vibrate at the same level as the situation. Reality will find the easiest way to match your energy level and beliefs. There is nothing as motivating as the **results** of our actions. We can tune our **MINDS** to specific streams of energy flow, finding what brings us peace of **MIND**. It's **all** within us—it requires self-acceptance, **knowing** your goals and boundaries, and understanding energy laws.

It's difficult for us to evaluate ourselves because we came into this world without payment, so we often don't **value** ourselves.

Yet, we are the most valuable of all we possess. Everything else must be earned. We create the life we vibrate with, shaping our world through the magnetic field of our thoughts. How we use this energy reflects in our results.

Only when we realise our worth do we begin to live.
Only when we recognise our uniqueness do we begin to create.
Only when we find love within ourselves do we begin to attract it.
And only when you light a flame inside yourself do you find true love.

Then, and only then, do we become successful, rich, and real. Only then do we know the giving love that brings true happiness—a love where there is no place for abuse, hatred, or evil.

When we act from abundance, more abundance comes. When we act from scarcity, more scarcity follows. Our psyche is complex, often supporting our traumas. We must be able to self-analyse.

We all have a need to be accepted and loved, to share and express our essence of love. The core value is within us. The energy of tension, control, competition, and protection are masculine (Yang) energies. The energy of acceptance, relaxation, beauty, and lightness are feminine (Yin) energies. These principles must be balanced within us.

As we mature, we play two equally strong roles as partners. A woman shows her strength through her femininity; a man through his masculinity. She supports and strengthens him and receives all that he has to offer. It is important to prioritise: first yourself, then your partner, then your children, and then all other things. Success comes from balance, not from changing roles. Disorder begins when things are out of order.

Release every burden, embrace life's pleasures, and join together in the joy of living. Irritation arises when we do not value or appreciate what we do. Self-doubt and fear are the most destructive vibrations for our future. We can serve the Source in every language, in any nation. Our MIND has two functions: memory and discernment. Thoughts are living energy, shaping our lives and those around us.

Our MIND can be a good servant when we are aware, but a bad master when left unchecked. Grievances are rooted in the past, and fears in the future. The present is goodness, the true light— being alive, feeling happy, and evolving spiritually. Goodness is the absence of internal conflict. What we see around us is only our interpretation. The present is the result of the past and the cause of the future.

First, we must learn to observe with acceptance, without conflict with the world. Then we can improve ourselves, learn to act, and eventually create. We start as spectators, become actors, and finally, the screenwriters of our lives. These are the levels to mastering spiritual principles.

Mental abuse, knowingly or unknowingly inflicted on oneself or others, is a sign of an unenlightened soul. A woman's power lies in her acceptance, sensuality, and softness. A man's power lies in his will, strength, and problem-solving abilities. Each woman carries 70% feminine and 30% masculine energy; each man carries 70% masculine and 30% feminine energy.

Just as a husband and wife complement each other, our conscious MIND leads, while our subconscious supports the conscious MIND'S beliefs and ideas. A man says, "Don't worry, I can do it. I can take care of it." A woman asks for advice, gently expresses her needs, and seeks help. She is sensitive, **emotional**, and in need of attention—attention, sympathy, support, and care are what she truly desires. She will not respond to a commanding voice. A man, logical and strong, protects her, creating a safe space where they can both be fulfilled.

But if she attacks or reproaches him, he will defend himself, worsening the situation. A man is wired to defend when challenged, and if he is attacked, he will accept the challenge. Instead of blame, ask for help or advice—he will always come to your aid. A man is destined to be generous, taking care of women, the elderly, and children. A mentally healthy man will always come to the rescue. He hears the meaning of what is said, while a woman hears the tone. She reacts to the timbre of his voice.

Paths of Wisdom

We must accept our place within our kind.
There is a structure, a role for each of us—
As sons and daughters, fathers and mothers.
Each must play their part.

When a man meets a mentally healthy woman,
It is a door to Heaven.
Likewise, when a woman meets a mentally healthy man,
She finds her path to Heaven.

But when opposites are imbalanced—
When a man meets an emotionally unstable woman,
It becomes a gateway to Hell.
When a woman encounters a mentally unstable man,
It is a path to despair.

Our ancestral values, our family line,
Hold significant power in our lives.
Those closest to us may trigger us the most.
But these moments are teachers,
Opportunities to learn, grow, and improve.
Change pays off when we treat it with respect.

Anger, greed, and lust are roads to Hell.
The most terrible force of distraction is resentment.
Respect for nature gives us physical health.
Respect for water brings vitality.
Respect for air and fire
Improves our emotional stability,
Our spiritual growth, and understanding.
Our MINDS are always at work,

Often unaware of their own thoughts.
We must learn to master our state of being,
To understand and apply this knowledge.
The oldest part of our brain,

The reptilian MIND, is challenging to manage.
It drives us to expand, but unchecked,
It leads us to greed and laziness.
Conflict destroys, but living in a meditative state,
In harmony with the Alpha rhythm,

Heals many diseases.

Our nervous and immune systems are intertwined.
When we interact, we change the object,
And the object changes us.
We know that observation alters reality,

And we must begin analyzing our thoughts,
Discarding the harmful and useless ones.
The way forward is through mindful action.
We are pure consciousness,
Our souls striving to live in bliss and harmony.

Happiness is achieved by perfecting our thoughts,
By forming intelligent patterns.
Our abilities and possibilities

Reside in the laboratory of our MINDS.
We don't have to believe blindly—
We can verify through our own experiences,
Becoming healthier in body, MIND, and spirit.

When we consume empty calories,
We gain no energy, only burden.
But when we nourish ourselves with high-energy food,
We fuel our lives with purpose.
The center of our being is our essential focus.

Perceiving and creating,
We harness and shape our thought patterns.

Our MINDS are powerful—
We can imagine holding a lemon,

See its yellow color,
Taste its sourness in our mouths.
But if we let suspicion take root,
It will grow, souring our relationships
And poisoning our interactions.

Scripture reminds us to keep our candle lit.
Oil symbolizes the presence and power of the Holy Spirit.
It represents wealth, abundance, health, energy—
The vital ingredients for a good life.
The seven churches, our seven energy centers,
Our chakras, must be aligned.

As Hebrews 9:14 explains,
The blood of Christ cleanses our consciences,
So that we may serve the living God.

For all who trust in Christ,
We are washed in His blood,
Freed from sin to serve Him fully.

Objective self-awareness arises
From comparing ourselves to others.
Subjective self-awareness comes
From recognizing that we are the source
Of our own perceptions and behaviors.

"Ask, and it will be given to you; seek, and you will find;
Knock, and it will be opened to you."
(Matthew 7:7-11)

Our mental state shapes our lives.

Information is energy, like food.

What we **focus** on, we digest,
And it affects our **emotional** and physical bodies.

The seven chakras symbolize energy centers,
Corresponding to nerves, organs, and spiritual areas
That impact our well-being.
Seven notes in harmony make a beautiful melody,
But the instrument must be tuned.
Many people, in cooperation,
Create an orchestra of life.

Spiritual and physical, connected through the soul—
Where soul decisions shape reality.
When we fall from grace,
We step out of the natural stream of evolution.
Devolution leads to darkness,
To **mental** states of conflict and despair.

But when we guide our **emotions** with wisdom,
When we balance our **MINDS** with conscious intent,
We become like a good captain,
Steering our lives with purpose and clarity.
The captain does not blame the weather,
But uses every resource wisely.
Observation and presence are constant,
A state of being that brings peace.

Knowledge brings ease,
Like learning to swim,
Allowing us to enjoy life while respecting its currents.

When we **focus** on goodwill,
On virtuous passion for ourselves and others,

We bring abundance, joy, and **love** into the world.
But acting from ignorance or victimhood
Creates fear and darkness.

When we treat others with sincerity,
When we discipline our **MINDS**,
We gain a peaceful state of **emotional** well-being.
Balanced actions follow,
And chapter by chapter,
We become more aware of our **inner** world.

A cup is just a **form**—
What we fill it with, poison or nectar, is our choice.
We can choose to remain stable,
In goodwill to ourselves and the world.
Every challenge is a lesson,
Every obstacle, a teacher.
There are no enemies, only opportunities to grow.

At some point, we understand—
When there is peace in our **MINDS**,
Our bodies heal with ease.
Don't chase happiness—become happy.
Don't run from problems—start solving them.

There was an old saying:

A fly returned from earth to the heavens.
They asked, "How was it there?"

The fly replied, "Poop, poop, poop!"

Then a bee returned from earth to the heavens.
They asked, "How was it there?"
And the bee answered, "Flowers, nectar, flowers!"

We must learn to notice our own nature.

Until we think guilty thoughts, we will judge others.
Until we suppress our true feelings, we can't be sincere with others.
Until we think unhealthy thoughts, we can't expect health.
Until we lie to others, we can't expect to know the truth.
Until we are jealous, there will never be enough.
Until we feed fear, fear will never leave us.
Until we think thoughts of lack, we will never feel abundance.
Until we think depressive thoughts, excitement, well-being, and
achievements will have no place.
Until we let go of feelings of misery and low self-worth, confidence
will disappear.

What we give, we will receive—sooner or later.

Our world is multifaceted, and we all belong, knowingly or
unknowingly, to this ever-changing river of life. When we
discipline our MIND and body, we heal our spirit. We become
healthy, and considerate of the quality of our thoughts and
speech, and aware of the results they produce. We can identify
falsehood instantly because we belong to life. We think clearly,
live with ease, and feel light. Knowledge is light, guiding us to
what is right—for us. But remember: what is right for you may
not be right for another.

Become a great example; don't push or pull others. Do what you **love**, and **love** what you do! Return to your natural state of being—thinking, feeling, and behaving in harmony, not in fear, but in **love**. Let's think constructively, uplifting and encouraging each other with sincerity, **love**, and unity.

Each of us is responsible for our own state of **MIND**.

Steadily and slowly, through time and **experience**, no matter where we are in life, we can always notice, focus, and be aware. Don't run 'from' fear—walk 'to' joy with courage! Be a source of joy; express joy, enjoy joy!

The world moves gradually and in spirals—upward, it's easy, wide, and clear; downward, it's heavy, blurry, and tense. If we don't pay attention to our **thoughts**, we may drift away from our natural, peaceful state of **MIND** and self-**growth**. Life is in constant motion, so we must stay sober, awake, and alert—like a driver on an adventure. Treat others according to their level of understanding, with passion and uplifting energy. Improve your **MIND**, body, and spirit. The world is one, and everyone has their truth, but **absolute** truth, the law, is the same for everyone. A fish thrives in **water** but dies on the table. What is good for one may not be good for another. Time, place, and situation are perceived differently depending on our state of **MIND**.

When we discipline our **MINDS** to stay happy, no matter what—whether people admire or gossip about us—we notice when manipulations arise, attachments to things or people, or opinions. We don't waste energy on low vibrational distractions that drain our natural creative abilities, leading to low self-esteem and depression. Each of us carries a cloud of information, interests, and **experiences**—a unique perspective through the lens of our own MIND. It's our responsibility to observe the workings of our MIND. What are we creating? How are we doing it?

The **essence** of our **inner** nature is like clean, **pure water**. When we are stable, sincere, and strong inside, our natural creativity flourishes. We become enlightened, and doors open to higher wisdom and harmony. A **wider** picture unfolds, full of exciting possibilities. Our **focus** and intention should always be to return to our healthy, natural state of enlightenment, to live easily, to prosper, to bring happiness, and to shine brightly for all!

To understand life's algorithms clearly, we must still our MINDS. We inherit patterns of behavior and perceptions from our family and society. The world we see **now** is the **result** of our previous thinking and behavior—cause and effect. Just as one must complete general education to enter university, so too must we cultivate ourselves to achieve our dreams.

The Bee and the Fly: A Lesson in Perspective

If you think you can, get ready—
Energy comes to those who believe,
Who align with the constructive,
Spiritual powers that fill their jars.

Walk your path with peace and steadiness,
Deep **inner** knowledge and **vision** perceived.
Rely on the natural peace within.

Memories, opinions,

Operate in faith, free from confusion.
Focus like a laser, and move on.
Give yourself space to process,
Plant **seeds** of **love** and knowledge,
Act steadily, balanced, aligned.

Doubts are sabotage,
Concise your decisions,
Keep your eyes crystal clear.
Plan with care, happiness, and joy.
Throne your wisdom, bless your world.
Close the circle of illusion, start the diffusion.
Illuminate, supply, and brighten with light.
Visualize the whole new you, settled.

A new phase of faith,
Receiving confirmation,
Nurture a rich, purposeful passage.
Transformation, **results** on a journey to permanence,
Certify and firm—genuine and true,
In control of your destiny,
Using **all** your gifts and talents.

The **source** gives us time,
The support system—universe.
Intentionally and deliberately,
Fortune comes from clearheaded decisiveness.
Know what's happening in and around you,
Manage energies by your will.
Heal and move creatively,
Steady a legacy of wealth,
Coming toward you through the cloud,

Clear, great, without greed,
A leaf in the wind—pure cause and effect.

Trap hot disappointments, release tension,
Resign from fear and letdowns,
You are the author of your dreams,
Detach and surrender,
Fuse real light and life.

Set and reach, enrich your goal,
A fairytale fire talent.
Say to yourself: Yes! I can!! I will!!!
I am able to heal any high hill!
Power, beauty, and pleasure,
There is so much more within.

Operate motivated by faith, not fear.
Congratulations, you are moving forward!!!
Live a joyful life, wisdom is freedom.
Access the path of inspiration! See and cure.
Avoid destructive assumptions.
Stay in your divine light—
The reward is worth the effort—
Quality and value in life's performance.
Stay thoughtful, know, and consider,
How your actions and words
Will affect others' feelings.

Life is a journey. There are times mind seasons. To fulfill our dreams, to get what we deserve, and to walk a certain way— we must be brave. Stop waiting. Break free from distracting energies. Take control of writing your own story.

Determine: "What is my life going to be like?"

The world is one, but we **all** walk in different shoes. When we control our MINDS, we control the quality and destination of our lives, bearing bright, healthy, beautiful fruits and satisfaction.

If we overfill or underfill, we won't enjoy the ride. If we don't know the measure, it won't benefit our health. What heals in the right proportion can be poison if overdosed. Know the measure and moderation in everything. Don't be pulled by **desires**. Don't be obsessed with temporary **material** things in this ever-changing world! Stay happy! Things come and go. Days pass and remain only in our memories.

Growing a fruitful tree takes time and care. There will be times to **water** it and weed around it. In time, it will bear **nurturing** fruits.

Life is a wave, a lifetime **experience**. It's not easy to navigate the ocean of life in a boat with **mental** holes. We must continuously keep balance and awareness on our journey. Keep yourself away from negative influences as you would from a bad smell.

Don't seek happiness outside—find it and build it inside. When we focus, it's like riding a horse. We are the rider, and the horse is energy. When we know where we're going, the universe sends powerful energies and **all** necessities our way.

The planets affect our energies—Sun for self, **Moon** for **emotions**, Mars for action, Venus for beauty, and so on. Every planet's position can be ascending or descending in our life chart. But no matter the influence, we can uplift and harmonize **all** aspects of our being, rolling easily, playfully with life.

Everything is energy, and when we understand this, we see that everything is an **expression** of energy—our art, our bodies, our voices. We can look around, interpret the energy surrounding us, and make changes.

When we suppress our **inner** feelings, negatively charged energy accumulates and condenses inside us, causing harm.

Every system has its rules—body, family, business, country. We already belong to a system, and when we enter a new one, we must follow its rules. Remember your place and role in the system. Perform your duties on time and be responsible. Respect the hierarchy and cooperate well with others. If we do well, we grow, improve our lifestyle, and gain self-confidence. People trust and rely on us, and we make real friends.

If we are in charge, we must have good character, fairness, and justice. Fairness means making judgments free from discrimination. We should **all** strive to practice fairness.

What happens if we don't follow the rules? Our bodies become diseased, our relationships fall out of harmony, and our work doesn't pay what we think we deserve—resentment.

Caring or loving unconditionally means serving others without expecting a reward. Respect others and make them feel joyful, comfort them, and be happy for their well-being. It's easy to do when we are admired and respected in return. But the key is to truly **love** from the heart, without forcing opinions or expecting anything in return.

Some people only respect those in higher positions or who pay them. It's important not to pretend. If you hate what you do and pretend, it's not productive. We must truly love what we do and do what we love.

There is a hierarchy in everything. We must respect our parents and care for them as they age. We must respect our teachers and our workplace, which pays for our needs, bills, and vacations. If we don't respect those who care for us, we block our blessings and stagnate our growth. We must respect the laws of the country we live in or travel to. If we don't, we get in trouble. Respect driving rules, or you'll get a ticket.

When we understand and follow universal laws, love is above all. There's a saying, "A little chick doesn't teach an old chicken."

Our children and pets teach us how to love unconditionally. They bring us joy, and it motivates us. We don't pretend; we truly love them. If we pretend, it becomes a burden, and neither we nor our pets are truly happy. Love is union, connection.

We also have to know our place, position, and responsibility. The head of a company has different responsibilities than others.

Some expect their partner to be like a parent—that is not the correct role. Or some behave with their partner as a parent or teacher. People play all kinds of roles—victim, tyrant, rescuer. A victim becomes a tyrant; a rescuer becomes a victim.

Egoism is doing everything for oneself, for others to admire. If they don't, the ego becomes angry, sad, judgmental, or jealous. These energies lead to madness—attachments and fears, likes and dislikes. We struggle to achieve things and then fear losing them. The only attachment we should have is to **self-discipline** our MIND, speech, and actions. Respect, honor, and glory will come naturally.

When we realize our **inner** world and clean our MINDS of debris, our **emotional** state harmonizes. Our life becomes a beautiful garden, and our physical health and vitality improve. Even our enemies may become our friends.

Navigating Life's Journey

Life is a journey, with its seasons and times. To fulfill our dreams, to claim what we deserve, we must be brave. Stop waiting. Break free from distractions. Take control of your story.

Ask yourself: *What is my life going to be like?* The world is one, but we each walk in different shoes. When we control our MINDS, we control the quality and destination of our lives. The **result**? Bright, happy, healthy, and satisfying fruits.

But balance is key. Overfill the tires, and the ride is rough; underfill, and it's unsteady. **Knowing** moderation in **all** things is wisdom. Don't be pulled by **desires** or obsessed with temporary **material** things in this ever-changing world. Stay happy! Things come and go. Days pass, leaving only memories.

Growing an apple tree takes time and care. There are seasons to **water** and weed, and in time, the tree will bear fruit. Life, too, is a wave, a lifelong **experience**. It's not easy to navigate the ocean of life in a boat full of holes. We must continually balance and steer with awareness. Keep away from negative influences, like avoiding a bad smell.

Don't seek happiness outside—find it, build it inside. When we focus, it's like riding a horse. We are the rider, and the horse is energy. When we set our sights on a destination, the universe sends powerful energies to help us along the way.

Planets affect our energies—Sun for self, **Moon** for **emotions**, Mars for action, Venus for beauty, and so on. These influences ebb and flow in our lives. Yet, no matter which planet is strong in our chart, we can uplift and harmonize **all** aspects, rolling easily with life.

Everything is energy. When we understand this, we see that everything—our character, art, body, and voice—is an **expression** of energy. We can look around, interpret the energies that surround us, and make changes.

When we suppress our **inner** feelings, negative energy accumulates and condenses within us, causing harm.

Every system has its rules—body, family, business, country. We belong to these systems and must follow their rules. Understand your place and role. Perform your duties responsibly. Respect your boss and cooperate with others. If you do well, you grow, gain confidence, and build trust.

If you are in charge, good character, fairness, and justice are essential. Fairness means making judgments free from discrimination. We should **all** strive for fairness.

What happens if we don't follow the rules? Our body suffers disease, our relationships fall out of harmony, and our work becomes unfulfilling.

Caring or loving unconditionally means serving others without expecting anything in return. Respect others, make them feel joyful, comfort them, and be happy for their well-being. True love comes from the heart, without forcing opinions or expecting payback.

Some people only respect those in higher positions or who pay them. But true respect and love are not transactional. We must LOVE what we do and DO what we love.

Hierarchy exists in everything. Respect your parents, care for them as they age. Respect your teachers. Respect your workplace, which provides for your needs. If you don't respect those who care for you, you block your blessings and stagnate your growth. Respect the laws of the land. If you don't, trouble follows. Respect the rules of the road, or you'll get a ticket.

When we understand and live by universal laws, we find that love is above all. As the saying goes, "A little chick doesn't teach an old chicken."

Children and pets teach us how to love unconditionally. They bring us joy, motivating us to care for them. True love is not pretentious. If we pretend, it becomes a burden, and neither we nor our loved ones are truly happy. Love is union, connection.

Know your place, position, and responsibility. The head of a company has different responsibilities than others. Some expect their partner to be like a parent, but that's not the right role. People play many roles—victim, tyrant, rescuer. A victim becomes a tyrant; a rescuer becomes a victim.

Ego-driven people do everything for themselves, seeking admiration. When they don't receive it, they become angry, sad, or jealous. These **emotions** lead to madness—attachments and fears, likes and dislikes. We struggle to achieve things and then fear losing them. The only attachment we should have is to **self-discipline** our **MIND**, speech, and actions. Respect, honor, and glory will come naturally.

When we understand our **inner** world and clean our **MINDS** of debris, our **emotional** state harmonizes. Life becomes a beautiful garden, and we achieve radiant health and well-being. Even our enemies may become our friends.

The first birth is physical; the second is spiritual.

The sun shines for all. A **seed** has the potential to grow into a strong, fruitful tree. From a fragile sprout to a stable tree takes time and effort. The same goes for our **MINDS**. When we train our **MINDS** to **focus** on true **value**, we bear good fruit. We attract the **right** people and situations by our vibrations. Problems become lessons to be learned.

Money can buy many things, but some things are beyond its reach.

When we grasp how energies function, we understand that our **focus** creates our destiny. To take control of our well-being, we must not feed negative energies. With **willpower**, we can reprogram our beliefs and attitudes. How we perceive ourselves and the world reflects back to us.

Pay attention to the details. Mastery and accuracy in small things prepare us for greater responsibilities.

Blaming others or the weather happens when we fall out of grace. We can't blame the cold if we aren't dressed warmly. We can't blame the forest if we enter it in high heels. When we stay busy with unnecessary things, remaining in a victim role, we can't be truly happy.

If we act insensitively, push others, or manipulate, our deeds will return to us with greater force. That is the universal law.

We cannot expect a pleasant fragrance from something rotten. Everything contains something. Subject and object are one.

Everything in the world already exists in **all forms** and varieties. We don't create; we illuminate what we **focus** on. We must understand that when we participate in unfair affairs or spread false information, we are "poisoning the **water** we drink." By our own ignorance, we poison our environment, our food, our earth, our relationships, and our trust.

We might blame God, the world, or others, but the truth is, we haven't learned how to live, how to think healthy thoughts. In the same city, some people live happily while others struggle. Our roots, our ancestors, and the lessons they taught us shape us. We have the power to reform, rewrite, and reprogram our story. We can live healthy, wealthy lives, radiating true abundance.

Love others as you **love** yourself.

Not every grown person is psychologically mature. Our subconscious MIND is like a deep ocean, containing all kinds of information. With our conscious MIND, we can choose, highlight, and direct ourselves toward our chosen path, revealing a wider view, knowledge, and understanding. This requires focus and attention.

Each of us has the potential to live harmoniously. Honesty with yourself is the key. When we accept ourselves without wearing masks, we pull ourselves out of illusions. The world becomes clearer, communications easier. Right knowledge builds a stable inner state, making the world around us bloom.

Any communication is an exchange of energy. We affect each other every time. Be aware of where your attention is.

A company or system was created by someone. But what about our bodies or the planetary system? Who created them? Our pets don't understand human society, but that doesn't mean it doesn't exist. The same goes for us; we often fail to realize the existence of a higher power.

In our awakening process, we use our conscious MINDS to correct ignorance. We interact with energies through our thoughts, words, and actions. Awareness frees us, constantly rewiring our neurons.

Emotions act fast, but we can evaluate before reacting. Animals react instinctively, but we can evaluate before speaking or acting. When we are led by emotions, we become slaves to them. We can take control of our lives by anticipating rather than reacting.

Training our nature, we rise above instinct. We got language, communication, and the ability to analyze and improve.

Many of us act on animalistic **desires**, unaware of our habits. We react with anger, suppress **emotions**, and create negative energies around us. Some animals live in luxury, while some people remain in low understanding of themselves, confused by the world.

Not everyone is lucky enough to be born into a balanced family. We get energy to charge our devices without understanding the **source**. We rely on others' expertise. The same goes for our planet, sun, and **moon**. There is a designer and operator, guiding us when we ask and listen.

But we are so conditioned by daily life that we fail to recognize this guidance. Instead, we waste vital energy feeding fears and battles, losing sight of our spiritual path.

We must see the illusion of our ego and embrace spiritual knowledge. Retreat from daily life and create space for introspection. Our ego craves attention, but we must not exaggerate our importance. We drain our energy when we exaggerate, making ourselves vulnerable.

Be observant, and don't let confusing **thoughts** spoil relationships. Spend energy **nurturing**, not on empty pursuits. Our **MIND** is a master at making excuses, weaving new karmic knots. Our level of **consciousness** determines our perception and life quality.

First, desire; then, believe and act to receive. After achieving something, analyze the process. How did **creation** work? Fear of loss drains our energy. Understand that what we **focus** on grows. Stop feeding destructive **thoughts** and nurture what you want to flourish.

You don't become a senior by age, but by quality. **Inner** qualities don't depend on age. A king might be younger than his warriors. Understand why you have an idea and spend your life force on it. Are you proving something to others, or seeking more and more? Our energy field determines our direction.

Confidence and decisiveness are necessary to win. Set great goals and go toward them. Your attention and time are limited, so invest them wisely. What you **focus** on, you acquire.

If we waste energy, it dissipates. When we respect something, it grows stronger. When we are small, we might not know the **value** of what we have. We might break something valuable, unaware of its worth.

Feeling small or rising above others is not the way to live. We are **all** unique, playing roles with different **desires** and necessities. Remember, we are learners and teachers to others. Respect those who teach you and guide the younger ones with patience and love.

As we clean and organize our space, we must also restructure our **MINDS**, letting go of old beliefs and discovering valuable treasures within. This is the process of mastering energy. Our **thoughts**, feelings, and actions **form** our song.

Our subconscious MIND is powerful, but with awareness and willpower, we can control it. We can reboot our system, cleaning out harmful beliefs and behaviors.

Our state of being affects everything. Positive energy develops us, negative energy distracts. To improve our behavior, we must improve our feelings, and to improve our feelings, we must improve our thinking.

Strong-willed intention, confidence, and resilience are the inner rod that supports us. If the results aren't what we want, it's a sign that our actions weren't right. Take responsibility for what happens.

The story of the scorpion and the turtle illustrates this well. The scorpion promised not to bite, but in the end, he did. We must be aware of others' true nature, no matter what they say.

Through awareness, responsibility, and the understanding of energies, we shape our journey. The way is forward, with clear eyes and a steady heart.

Path to True Wisdom and Fulfillment

When we do what is right, merely because it is right, without love, we risk becoming envious of those who truly love doing what is right. Those who act out of genuine love have no competition. They don't seek approval or validation; they simply follow their heart.

Assessing what is happening in our lives is our own responsibility. Happiness, wisdom, and self-realization are within our reach.

We have the **inner** power to change our destiny, to erase old, false beliefs, and to create new, beneficial ones for ourselves and the world around us.

Guilt and shame, whether for ourselves or others, cloud our judgment. Everyone walks their own path; we cannot walk it for them. Our first task is to distinguish between what truly matters, guided by love—not the **love** we often think of, but a constant, all-encompassing love. This **love** instructs, encourages, and nourishes without aggression, leading with **wisdom** rather than force.

Helping out of pity is not the same as supporting someone out of understanding. When we choose to help because we can and because we see an opportunity to improve a situation or a life, we act from a place of strength and compassion.

Our journey began long before this lifetime. On a soul level, we came here to forget and then to remember who we truly are. When we believe life ends with the body, we cannot comprehend the true meaning and power within us. We think our parents created us, but they merely facilitated our physical **form**. The real **creation** lies beyond their understanding, governed by a higher power.

This higher power is the root of our existence, the **source** of true **vision**, knowledge, and support. The sun, the seasons, **all** are ruled by this force. We can seek wisdom from it, striving to align with its qualities and oneness. Though we call this force by different names—God, Allah, Shiva, Buddha—the **essence** remains the same.

Understanding the deeper meanings within scriptures, written in parables and myths, requires effort. Each of us must undertake the intensive work of self-discovery to find peace and purpose.

As we grow, we recognize that the same eye has been observing the world through our changing bodies since childhood. We are beyond space and time, connected psychophysically and spiritually. Our purpose or goal gives us the energy to walk toward our dreams with grace and ease, without attachment.

We have two great needs: to love and to be loved. We find meaning in life through creative work and through love, guided by the attitudes we adopt. True fulfillment comes not from the pursuit of pleasure or power, but from seeking meaning and understanding our state of being. Walking through life with responsibility, paying attention to the small steps and details, leads to self-realization.

Frustration and emptiness signal a need for deeper comprehension. Life's challenges often teach us the most profound lessons. Just as sunlight pierces through space to reach Earth, our soul breathes through our MIND into consciousness. As darkness vanishes in the presence of light, so too does fear when we are connected to the Creator, the source of harmony and fulfillment.

Self-discipline is essential. When we grow spiritually clean, we see wisdom flourish around us. Our connections with others become supportive, bringing joy to ourselves and those we love. As we learn to shine selflessly, universal powers flow through us, revealing our true spiritual purpose and vitality.

In wisdom, we rejoice in the happiness of others. We gain **emotional** stability and a sense of fulfillment. **Emotional** anguish—trauma, grief, sorrow, anxiety, fears—melts away like ice in the sun. Renewed energy flows through us and the world around us, bringing healing.

When we **focus** on the quality of service we provide to others, we receive appreciation in return, gaining the wings to create even more good in the world. However, when we act only for **personal** gain, disregarding others' well-being, we create a sphere of aggression, pressure, and insincerity that leads to fear and disharmony.

Everything is governed by universal energies. Small parts build large structures, and in connection, they serve a greater purpose. Little things matter, and little steps lead to great achievements. To build something valuable, practical, or stable requires a great idea that benefits and enriches all. Generosity is the foundation of prosperity.

The energy of **love** is giving. First, we give thoughtful attention to a great idea, get excited, and face challenges as lessons. Then, we receive the **results** we planted. Doubts and despondency only hinder us. Complaining about life or judging others makes us bitter and insecure, separating us from the world and others.

We create our **inner** world by shaping our relationships with ourselves and others through our attention and **intentions**. Our lifestyle, the people around us, our health, and our appearance reflect our character. The outer world echoes back to us what we have nurtured within.

Our MIND has two main functions: accepting or rejecting. Our five senses—taste, hearing, sight, touch, and smell—serve the MIND. The MIND is like a central server, regulating our feelings. When we like something, we say, "I want it." When we don't, we say, "I don't want it." Happiness on a physical level is fleeting, but mental happiness is deeper. Our internal value system determines our quality of life.

The MIND delights in ideas, but there is something higher than the MIND —willpower, freedom to choose, memory, knowledge, and the ability to plan and analyze. When we focus our willpower on what truly matters, we prioritize wisely.

Our body takes—food, water, air—like a child. Our spiritual part is like a parent to our physicality. When we develop the habit of controlling our emotions, we become aware of our thoughts and the patterns woven into our lives. Ignorance blocks the subtle areas of life. We must strive to know what we need to achieve.

When we take and take, we become like a black hole, never satisfied, attached to forms, and led astray from true relationships, wisdom, and abundance. When we perceive ourselves only as physical beings, we consume without understanding. Recognizing that we are created in the image of the Creator means we have the power to create our paradise or hell here on Earth.

Following the rules of daily life and natural spiritual laws directly impacts our destiny. Failure to comply with these laws leads to destruction or fatality. Each of us can analyze and find out where we stand. Are we breaking any laws of life? What force guides us—love or fear?

Recurring situations in life are lessons to be learned. Resentment, anger, and dissatisfaction may stem from early childhood experiences.

The sun represents the father, and the moon represents the mother. These energies influence the earth. The left side of our body is feminine, and the right side is masculine. If we are in conflict with our father, it may manifest as problems on the right side of our body.

Masculine power is the energy that affirms, expands, and achieves. It is determination, dynamism, and inner confidence. When contact with the sun is broken, a person becomes insecure, unable to achieve anything in life. Without energy to act, they become aggressive or domineering.

Lunar energy, like moonlight, calms, cools, and harmonizes. A woman's natural faithfulness to her partner brings beauty, aesthetics, and harmony to the home and family. Her internal harmony is harmony for the entire family. Just as the left and right arms are connected, so too are all parts of the body. One hand does not fight the other.

As parents, we are the first and most fundamental influence on our children's psychological health. How we use our energy is a matter of choice. Behind everything is the law and loving force of the universe. We are here to learn, recognize lessons, and return to our true inheritance and natural state of abundance.

What we attach ourselves to binds us. The future will unfold based on the meaning we give and the attention we pay. The future can be bright and easy if we combine spiritual wisdom with the latest technology in ecological ways for all.

When we recognize that we are part of an everlasting, ever-living consciousness in temporary bodies, we can participate in building a beautiful self, family, and world. We start to understand that anything is possible. We are units in the universal web of consciousness, influencing each other's lives.

The Creator is our main energy source, and life is the screen on which our energy plays out. We attract ideas, memories, and attachments that pull us into different scenes. Dependence and attachment can lead us astray.

In theaters, many rooms show different movies—comedy, adventure, horror. Life is like a movie theater; scenes and actors change, but the screen remains the same.

When we fall from grace, we may chase money but lose our true inner connection and the people we love. We may engage in ignorant or disrespectful relationships that contradict natural laws. If we only take and never give, we become like a foreign cell in the body.

Life energy, filtered through our core beliefs, supports our ideas. It's like our home, where we use energy for different purposes. Companies use multiple devices depending on their goals. Each of us has a unique purpose to serve, spending and expressing ourselves. It may be hard at the beginning, but with understanding and knowledge, it becomes easier.

We must learn not to blame others or ourselves. Learn to be happy, no matter what!

We live in a world where everyone owns media. We live in a modern technological world where information is available to all. You and I live in a single ecosystem, united humanity. We are responsible for our planet and the situation here. Changing our thinking paradigm changes our destiny. Because today, we have the opportunity to influence, we influence each other.

Crisis or pain is feedback from the world. We must understand the meaning that life gives us. When we develop a loving perception of the world, the world opens up to us.

Our perception and view of the world determine our destiny. Influencing others through offense or manipulation leads to recurring suffering and leaves a damaging effect. When our intent is to consciously help others, we create an environment where pure, real nature, talents, and qualities manifest naturally. The ecology of our thinking is fundamental in all relations and spheres of life.

Existential analysis is necessary to find our own ridiculous way of existence. We must identify and transcend the most significant problems of our time. The nature of truth reveals itself in giving and receiving. False associations and attempts to extract pleasant sensations lead to illusions and difficulties. This distortion of perception makes it difficult to access our consciousness and confuses us.

Thinking about past dramas with resentment or regret drains our energy and increases cortisol levels. Constant stress affects the adrenal glands and overall well-being. Shift attention away from the past and **focus** on the **future** you want to create.

When we ask constructive questions and **focus** on new dreams or projects, we find meaning and purpose. Serotonin levels harmonize, bringing focus, **emotional** stability, happiness, and calm.

Our condition affects how we feel in this world. Our feelings influence our **emotions** and reactions, which in turn determine how we vibrate in the world. This vibration frequency draws events to us that match our **inner** state. If there is a victim inside, it will always attract the executioner.

Analyze **all** aspects of your life to gain a clearer picture of where you are and where your efforts are needed. When we **focus** on something, a system opens up, providing the signs and tools we need. We catalyze each other.

Good, holy, and beautiful things lead to liberation. You were born to create. This understanding is a gift for those who grasp it. **Absolute love** casts out **all** fear.

I Am Enough

"I am. I am here. I am enough."

"The people who live poorly are those who spend their entire lives just planning to live."
"When we do good for others, the kind appreciate it, the indifferent forget, and the arrogant become more arrogant."

"If someone betrays another for you, don't tie your life to them—sooner or later, they will betray you too."

"Fear the tears of the one you've wronged, for when they ask God for help, He will answer."

"Don't pray for an easy life; pray for the strength to handle any difficulty."

"Your life depends 90% on you and only 10% on circumstances, which are themselves 99% dependent on you."

"If they spit at your back, it means you're ahead."

"When you find yourself in a hole, the first thing to do is stop digging."

"No one can change, but everyone can become better."

"The more you say, the less people remember."

"When you realize you've made a mistake, don't hide it—correct it quickly."

"People are lonely because instead of building bridges, they build walls."

"It is not external circumstances but your thoughts that make you happy or unhappy. Control your thoughts, and you control your happiness."

"Communicate less with those who burden you with their problems. Offer help but keep your distance. Strive to connect with positive, energetic people, those on your wavelength."

"Stabs in the back often come from those you protect with your chest."

"I always look for the good in people; they reveal the bad themselves."

"Don't fear winter after autumn, but be cautious of autumn before winter."

"Human nature is such that it is hard to learn goodness but easy to lean toward evil. We become like those with whom we surround ourselves."
"If you can't forgive others, you can't forgive yourself."
"In a quarrel, it's not you they attack but your energy, which they lack. Learn to restrain yourself, and many problems will solve themselves."
"No one can let you down if you don't depend on anyone."
"Everyone lives as they want and pays for it themselves."
"When trouble strikes, you find out who your true friends are."
"Be aware of people with envy, greed, stinginess, and arrogance in their hearts."

If we actively work on ourselves, we can quickly develop all the right qualities. But to do this, we must act decisively.

Here's something to consider: If someone offends me, should I be offended?
If someone offends me, should I get angry and seek revenge?
If someone steals from me, should I be angry?
When I am humiliated, do I need to humiliate others in return?

We must understand that our personal spiritual journey begins with self-improvement—soul mastery, then MIND, and finally body. The soul is strong when it is connected to higher spiritual wisdom. Stand in your light, stand in your love, stand strong in your purpose. Love is the greatest unifying power in the universe. We work on our physical actions and behaviors, but it is even more important to work on our inner thought processes. These unseen processes shape our lives, even if they are hidden beneath a mask, sometimes even hidden from ourselves.

When we learn to guide our thoughts, to deliberately delete what no longer serves us, and to implement new patterns that inspire and uplift, we transform our lives.

What is depression? Have you ever thought about the thoughts that swirl through your MIND, day after day? It is our greatest responsibility to analyze, reset, and be aware of the creative power of our MINDS. We are responsible for our creations. By taking stock of our state of being, the situations we find ourselves in, and the people around us, we can guide our lives in the direction we desire. Whatever has happened until now, whatever you find yourself in, can be reformed, restructured, remodeled, reprogrammed, and reimagined.

When it's cold, we seek warmth. When it's dark, we turn on the light. By learning to regulate and normalize the extremes of duality, we can achieve unity and harmony.

Become what you want to see in the world. Spiritual growth means cleansing our character, developing the habit of accepting the world as it is, and maintaining a happy state of MIND. This leads to peace of MIND, as our soul enjoys a harmonious ride through life. When we harmonize our mental and emotional bodies, our soul and spirit unite. The soul, connected to the spirit, knows the true path. The MIND is the filter, the willpower the rider, the body the cart, and the life forces the horses, guided by discipline and purpose.

But when we become obsessed with material things, the MIND loses sight of the soul-body-spirit connection. We go astray, lose our sense of direction, our purpose, and our perception, becoming delusional, deceiving ourselves, and our true being.

At this point, we **experience** negative **emotions** and **thoughts**, blaming gods, circumstances, and those around us—like someone being driven astray by wild horses.

All our attachments, **desires**, and struggles stem from ignorance or a lack of understanding of self and the universal energies. Lust, anger, envy, violence, impatience, greed, delusions, dependence on others, jealousy, pride, doubt, and disgust— these are the **seeds** of an impure **MIND**.

Everything is available in **all** shapes and **forms**, but it is up to us to choose wisely, to live intentionally, and to cultivate a life of love, wisdom, and harmony.

The Power of Love and Creation

The Creator is all-encompassing energy, the power of love— the greatest unifying force in the universe, structuring life itself. When we feel a lack of love, we must first look within to see if we are generating, vibrating, and giving love. When we radiate love, when we are ready to **love** and wish well for all, we attract similar energy. First, we must become love, believe in it, and then we will see and enjoy its blessings. Apply this truth and thrive. Dwell in happiness, do and wish well for all, and flourish. Everything we seek is within us, readily available.

Understanding this is the key to ceasing our endless pursuit of pleasure and happiness in external things. It **all** resides within. The cause and effect, from **inner thoughts** to outer **form**, is how **creation** manifests—from the invisible to the visible world. As the Bible says in Matthew 6:10, "Thy **kingdom** come. Thy will be done on earth, as it is in heaven." Our thoughts, repetitive feelings, and actions shape our results and habits.

An architect has a great idea for a project, and with focus, he brings it to life. There is no time for blame or judgment when we are busy with our own creations. Understanding universal laws makes us examples for others, enabling us to help and support them sincerely in this wondrous journey called life. Devotion to purity on our path is essential for generating sustainable prosperity and success.

When we ask, "How can I be fit and healthy? How may I be more abundant? What can I do to achieve a certain state of being?" we open doors to health and radiance that echo and reflect in our lives. But first, we must serve with love and seek wisdom. Intelligence alone is not enough; wisdom opens to those who are pure in heart and intent. True knowledge expands our intellectual MIND, consciousness, and overall well-being. We have free will to choose; the spirit does not pressure the soul. A pure attitude toward the world and a right relationship with our own energies are necessary. Living in attunement with spirit, in harmony, allows us to maintain a high quality of character.

It's not enough to say, "Well, that's who I am." We must strive for more. Just as there are standards for a manager, we too must meet the standards required of us. Those with influence and authority must follow high standards because they are watched by others, especially the younger generations.

No one forces us to become pure. At some point, we naturally understand it, just as we naturally choose clean water over stale. Everyone desires happiness, but what we build here is temporary. Happiness found in people, pets, or possessions is fleeting. A child's joy in a bike will fade as they grow, just as the bike will no longer fit them. If we tie our happiness to business or weather, it too will change. We must learn that nothing and no one can touch our natural source of inner joy. It is all in our MIND; we can always adjust, dust off, and do what is best in the moment—enjoying and being happy, no matter what.

Life is a fast-flowing river, constantly changing. Wrong, limiting beliefs are what keep us from achieving our natural state of joy. We chase happiness, hooked on fear, running from situations, fearing failure, suffering to hold on, afraid to lose. When we get stuck in negative thinking, we attract more of it. Like a parent cleaning a mess, we must deal with it, doing our best, detached from anger. Fascinations can be like traps—bewitching us, only to swallow us whole.

Be aware of your feelings, your state of MIND, and the people you surround yourself with. Ask yourself: What am I doing, and why? Where will it lead? What could be the outcome? Can I say no when necessary? Knowing where we're going and what we're doing is essential. Every detail matters. When we clean up our inner world, our outer world will reflect similar energies: good people, beautiful surroundings, and positive situations. We live what we choose to feed and water.

Human and divine principles operate on different levels. Some follow the law of the jungle, some don't obey any law, and others follow divine rules and laws. Liberation from the MIND'S suffering and false restrictions is true freedom.

What we reject and hate is often what we project, unconsciously creating what we dislike. The sun shines from above, and **growth** occurs from the ground up, with plants striving toward the light. Without spiritual connection, it's like a plant without light or a computer without WiFi. The same thing can bring pleasure or pain, depending on the circumstances. Chasing pleasures leads to running from pain.

In the spiral of life, we move up or down—up toward the light or down into the heavy, linear existence. Understanding the rules makes life easier. Breaking them brings consequences.

Our bodies are sensing devices; they don't lie. The MIND filters our experiences. Liberation comes when we free ourselves from the MIND'S suffering and false limits.

What we project outward is what we receive. A disconnected spirit is like a plant without light. We must manage our energies, not let them control us. We are capable of controlling, choosing, and directing our thoughts; our emotions and actions will follow accordingly.

Remember, we live in a world where everything is energy. When we understand this, we stop chasing pleasure and happiness externally and begin to create it from within. We are the architects of our lives, and the universe responds to our intentions. Align with love, wisdom, and purpose, and watch as your life transforms into the beautiful creation it was always meant to be.

Galaxy Song (By Monty Python, 1983)

Whenever life gets you down, Mrs. Brown
And things seem hard or tough
And people are stupid, obnoxious, or daft
And you feel that you've had quite enough
Just remember that you're standing
On a planet that's evolving
And revolving at nine hundred miles an hour
That's orbiting at nineteen miles a second, so it's reckoned
The sun that is the **source** of all our power
The sun and you and me and all the stars that we can see
Are moving at a million miles a day
In an outer spiral arm, at four hundred thousand miles an hour
In the galaxy we call the Milky Way
Our galaxy itself contains a hundred billion stars
It's a hundred thousand light-years side to side
It bulges in the middle, six thousand light-years thick
But out by us, it's just a thousand light-years wide
We're thirty thousand light-years from galactic central point
We go 'round every two hundred million years
And our galaxy is only one of millions of billions
In this amazing and expanding universe
The universe itself keeps on expanding and expanding
In all of the directions it can whizz
As fast as it can go, at the speed of light, you know
Twelve million miles a minute and that's the fastest speed there is
So remember, when you're feeling very small and insecure
How amazingly unlikely is your birth
And pray that there's intelligent life somewhere out in space
'Cause there's bugger all down here on Earth

Realize ~ real eyes.

Olena lives in the beautiful state of California, finds inspiration in the natural beauty surrounding her, from the ocean to the mountains and forests she loves to explore. Her creative passions include cooking, music, poetry, and dance, which allow her to express herself and connect with others. She is deeply invested in understanding the connection between our mental state and overall well-being, analyzing how thought patterns influence emotional and physical health. Through her insights, Olena aims to share how cultivating positive thinking can lead to a healthier, more balanced life, benefiting both body and mind.